SUBMISSIVE TRAINING

How To Be A Better, Naughtier Submissive For Your Dominant Partner and 30 Hottest Sexual Scenarios with Illustrations

Joshua Matthew

Text Copyright © 2017 Joshua Matthew

All rights reserved. No part of this guide may be reproduced in any form without permission in writing from the publisher except in the case of brief quotations embodied in critical articles or reviews.

Legal & Disclaimer

The information contained in this book is not designed to replace or take the place of any form of medicine or professional medical advice. The information in this book has been provided for educational and entertainment purposes only.

The information contained in this book has been compiled from sources deemed reliable, and it is accurate to the best of the Author's knowledge; however, the Author cannot guarantee its accuracy and validity and cannot be held liable for any errors or omissions. Changes are periodically made to this book. You must consult your doctor or get professional medical advice before using any of the suggested remedies, techniques, or information in this book.

Upon using the information contained in this book, you agree to hold harmless the Author from and against any damages, costs, and expenses, including any legal fees potentially resulting from the application of any of the information provided by this guide. This disclaimer applies to any damages or injury caused by the use and application, whether directly or indirectly, of any advice or information presented, whether for breach of contract, tort, negligence, personal injury, criminal intent, or under any other cause of action.

You agree to accept all risks of using the information presented inside this book. You need to consult a professional medical practitioner in order to ensure you are both able and healthy enough to participate in this program.

TABLE OF CONTENTS

INTRODUCTION

Since "50 Shades of Grey", more and more minds have opened themselves up into the BDSM world and I would assume that if you have bought this book, you're here to learn a bit more.

At some parts, do note that this book would definitely overlap with examples from the other aspects of BDSM, such as Bondage, Discipline and Sado-masochism. The primary content would still however, focus on Dominant-submissive relationships and more specifically - on how you can be a better, naughtier submissive for your Dominant partner.

This book will primarily consist of three main components:

1) Basic knowledge about what it means to be a submissive, how a submissive mindset is formed, why you should become a submissive as well as guidelines to keep yourself safe if and when you decide to take on this somewhat taboo activity.

2) You will also learn what to say or do to become a better submissive in order to please your dominant partner more through conditioning, rules and protocols as well as tips to increase pain tolerance if your Dom is a sadist.

3) Finally, the book will provide 30 sexual scenarios for you and your dominant partner to explore and apply for the best Dominant/submissive - D/s experience.

Let's get started shall we?

WHAT IS SUBMISSION?

According to Merriam-Webster, **submission** is defined as the action or fact of accepting or yielding to a superior force; or to the will or authority of another person.

As such, a **submissive** would be one who desires or occupies a situation or role of deliberate, consensual subjection, granting another person the power to exert control over him or her.

In contrast, the other person would be **Dominant**[1].

Dominance and submission, or D/s, typically involves a series of actions, practices and routines the submissive follows to please the Dominant. A D/s connections are not always sexual

---

[1] Note: It is common for writers to capitalize the "D" in Dominant but leave the "s" in lowercase for the submissive. This is extended to referring to the Dominant in capitalization (e.g. His, Hers, Him, Her, He, She) to make it clear that they are referring to a Dominant, and a submissive using lowercase i (instead of capital I) when writing about himself or herself to make it clear that they are submissive.

in nature, as you will come to learn in the following sections. A D/s relationship could also be physical or nonphysical.

Certain relationships between Dominants and submissives cross into the severe physical realm of sadomasochism (commonly referred to as S&M, S-M or S/M), which involves the giving and receiving of pleasure from acts involving the receipt or infliction of pain or humiliation.

In nonphysical D/s relationships, interactions can take place anonymously in a virtual setting like a phone call, text or email. But regardless of whether it is sexual or non-sexual, physical or nonphysical, both parties in D/s are usually gratified and/or aroused by either mastering over others or being mastered over, and they do so consensually.

Submission can apply to several aspects of life and can be classified into three main levels. However, be aware that within these three main branches, there are a total of nine categories and levels of submission, which have been detailed within and referenced by several books that discuss D/s relationships.

Type 1: The Sexual Submissive

A sexual submissive is one who goes into a D/s relationship for their own sexual gratification. In other words, it is purely for sex and once these needs are met - these submissives do not feel any need to submit any other personal control to their partner.

Type 2: The Psychological Submissive

On another level, the psychological submissive typically includes masochists who are in a D/s relationship because they desire pain and/or humiliation. Similar to masochists, the psychological submissive derives sexual gratification from their own pain or humiliation.

Type 3: The Natural Submissive

Also known as the "true submissive", these are people who are said to be born with submissive tendencies and have the natural inclination to please other people This circumstance surpasses sexual gratification, which means natural submissives will eagerly relinquish control to their Dominant without any conditions (or very minimal ones).

You will, of course, be the one to decide what kind of submissive you want to be. There's no such thing as the 'best type' of submissive - you could even try out being all three types - though being a "natural submissive" may be something you're born with rather than something you nurture over time.

However, that doesn't mean it is impossible. With this book, you'll explore in greater detail the psychology of becoming a submissive.

Take a look at this excerpt, about how a submissive thinks his/her role should be at the end of the day:

"Submission is giving control of myself to another. That's the technical definition anyway. But it is so much more than that. It is emotional and psychological way before it is physical. Submission isn't a want for me, it's a need, and it isn't something I do just for kicks or sexual thrills. It is what I have to do. It is an integral part of who I am. Submission means to me that I strive to please my Master above myself, even if I'm not really in the mood.

It isn't just submitting to the pleasurable things but submitting/accepting the not-so-pleasurable things as well, that do or will please Him. It isn't all sex, though that is included. It is service as well. For me, it is more the service than the play. Things like making the bed, cleaning the house, getting his coffee, and other household chores making our home a welcoming place for Him to come home to. It's wearing the clothes He likes seeing on me. It's striving to be the best I can be for Him.

Submission which flows naturally from to me my Master is what brings me the greatest personal joy but can also bring emotional pain as well. It is knowing, even during times of confusion, deep inside that I belong to my Master no matter what."

The Psychology Of Being Submissive

So *why* exactly does one submit or want to submit?

There are arguably different reasons depending on one's lifestyle, primarily. This could be due, but not limited, to:

- religion

- sexual gratification

- an innate desire to be subservient

- curiosity

- therapy

Once again, it comes down to personal choice and lifestyle, which would determine a person's reason for being a submissive.

To gain a better understanding as to what goes on in the head of a submissive, here are some excerpts written from Dorothy Hayden, MBA, CSW, CAC - a Private Psychotherapist from New York City who specializes in sexual health.

Let's explore in greater detail what your reasons may be for becoming a submissive.

"A number of years ago, in connection with my work with sexual addiction, a number of lifestyle submissives started coming to me for treatment. Some of these people were extremely hesitant to discuss their reasons for seeking therapy; they were so ashamed of their fantasies and behaviors that it took years of working with them until I knew their real names or their telephone numbers.

Patients who were able to be forthcoming about their masochistic behaviors and fantasies were as confused as I was. One of my patients, giving me a written masochistic fantasy after months of resistance, said, "Here it is. This is what I came to therapy for. It's terrible. It's sick. It's wonderful. I hate it; it's my favourite fantasy. I can't stand it, I love it. It's disgusting. I don't want to stop it."

Hayden found her journey through the realm of S/M an invaluable learning experience, while simultaneously puzzling.

She found that her clients wanted happiness yet they also wanted to evade suffering. They sought to sustain and build the control they felt they had over themselves and their environment. They also desired to improve their self-respect, self-esteem and prominence. It's a confusing paradox based on the aforementioned principles.

It is said that human nature is wired with the instincts to avoid pain, maintain control, and increase esteem, and yet masochists purposefully seek pain, submission and humiliation.

"I heard stories of whips, canes, racks, cock-and-ball torture, dripping wax on naked skin, electronic devices designed to deliver just the right amount of pain, the difficulty of finding the right mistress, and the surprising number of "dungeons"[2] that existed within a few blocks' radius of my mid-town office. Time and again, men would talk of the frustration of being unable to entice their wives or partners, who found these sexual activities to be perverse, into engaging in the sexual behaviors that they most longed for."

The funny thing was that these submissives were not inferior or unsuccessful in any way by social standards. They are usually individuals with significant amounts of inner strength, coping abilities, and an ethical understanding of personal responsibilities. Much of these masochistic sexual activities

---

[2] A "dungeon" is the physical place where a BDSM activity takes place. They are also commonly referred to as a "playspace" or "club".

occur among powerful politicians, influential judges and other successful and formidable men.

After listening to her clients across the years, Hayden found masochism to be more of a metaphor for the circumstances in which a person's psyche expresses the extent of its suffering and fervor.

She found that one of the core reasons to becoming a submissive is **the deeper yearning** to be communicated with, understood and invited into a safe place. For example, the common rape fantasy could simply mean wishing to be discovered, identified and penetrated in a way that would make that person feel real, or as one analyst stated, "to come into being."

Beyond the desire to yield oneself and give way to a 'truer' being, masochistic operations have deeper significance, a way of striving towards the fulfilment of a very present human desire for fantasy play. Fantasies allow for the full spectrum of emotions within circumstances that range from controlling, being controlled, teasing and pleasing, allowing participants to reach something beyond the boring day-to-day life. This is the exit route from normal reality, which is actually essential for the average human being.

Lastly, in staying consistent with its contrary nature, masochism is not as concerned with being in a state of weakness as it is the state of **surrender, reception, and responsiveness**. Masochism delves into the idea of opening oneself completely to an experience, often moving in opposition to the egocentric, prudent, and competitive society at large. Power can be a horrific burden, and releasing the pressures that come with it can be a way to gain relief. In fact, Carl Jung regarded this dark, unconscious faction of the human mind not as a disease, but as a necessary component that keeps the psyche healthy. Embracing this is believed to provide a more complete sense of **self-awareness, self-acceptance, and a more complete sense of vitality**.

Why Become A Submissive?

So what are your goals? Are they the same as other submissives i.e.

1) to be reached, known and accepted in a safe environment,

2) to fulfil a human need for fantasy,

3) to embrace a sense of surrender and self-acceptance,

...or are you just doing this because you're pressured into doing so?

This is where a line is drawn, and ultimately, you shouldn't be forced into doing something you're not comfortable with.

Should you be forced to do something that's not of your own accord, then it's not too far off from **rape**.

The reasons why individuals choose to be submissive fluctuate considerably, depending on the individual. Some are submissive just to add an extra zing to their personal lives. Others might feel a profound psychological need that drives them inexorably toward submissive behaviors.

SUBMISSIVE TRAINING

This chapter will explore in greater detail as to what you may find acceptable as reasons to participate in BDSM[3] or more specifically, to become a full-fledged submissive.

For most people, wanting to become a submissive may just be their solution to spicing up their sex lives - treading into unchartered waters, basically. These are just people who want to try something new, because they haven't done this before and want to see if it's something they would like.

We can actually consider this to be of a somewhat nature-versus-nurture debate, in the sense that there are people who are born with these fetishes.

And there are those who later consider being in D/s relationships, usually becoming interested or influenced only after being exposed to a stimulus. Curiosity is the first step down to the path of awakening, after all.

We'll be addressing the ones who were naturally like this, or who have found their "true selves" through trial and error.

---

3 BDSM is a variety of roleplaying or erotic practices involving bondage, discipline, dominance and submission, and sadomasochism.

When you first grasp that you are having fantasies that meet the guidelines of fetishism or BDSM, the first reaction may be denial, self-disgust and even self-hate.

However, if this is a lifestyle that you truly feel you connect with, you will inevitably have to learn to overcome the embarrassment towards those desires. Suppressing your inner desires could lead to bad outcomes, such as poor mental health or worse - depression.

As such, you'll have to grind through a few stages towards achieving understanding and acceptance, which is the level you must be at to move forward. Realization comes first. This is when you uncover your proclivity towards particular behaviors. While it is not unusual for many to unearth the truth at an early age - even childhood -, others may not come to realize their preferences until much later. One thing that's for sure is that it is quite common for the first detection to be met with immediate denial and shock, with people usually having trouble believing something like this could ever happen to them.

In order to find out exactly what you are, you proceed with the second stage - which is research. You soon realize that there are many others just like you, and that it's all completely okay. You start to entertain thoughts of being subservient, tortured or humiliated. Or maybe you're a Dominant, and you start having fantasies about taking over control of someone else.

When you find out what you like and don't like, you go to stage three - experimentation. You seek people who are like-minded in their desires, but with opposing roles. You ascertain that your search would lead to a D/s relationship that is safe and conducive for you to cultivate and fulfil this different type of desire.

By then, you would have accepted that you in fact are not abnormal, and your desires are not unnatural. As you grow more active in *this* world, you'll become more comfortable investigating the depths of your sexuality, until you find that your initial fear has turned into excitement over a great learning experience.

The more you discover and find that you like becoming a submissive, the more successful you become at finding **the right reasons** for becoming a submissive.

Having said that, it's important to remember that D/s is not some sort of cure-all for the woes of life. Yes, D/s is fun and can be safe, but it's not going to make you younger or happier. You may have a lovely time in the dungeon and you might even enjoy pushing your boundaries and edges the entire time, but you will not fix problems that happen outside of the bedroom by heading down this direction.

Here are some reasons why **you shouldn't become a submissive**:

It Will Not Improve a Relationship

Maybe you lost some spice in your relationship, but there's a fine line between some kinky sex and going into D/s. Most of the time, it's actually just having better communication between your partner and talking about what is happening in your relationship. Iron out the kinks first before engaging in kinkier sex.

It Will Not Cure Depression

Pleasing a person may feel like a good thing, so becoming a submissive may automatically seem like the ultimate solution to making yourself feel good. Unfortunately, this kind of mentality is flawed and depending on the Dominant you find yourself with - you might just get taken advantage of, which could lead you into an even bigger downward spiral. The best thing to do is to seek the help of a trained therapist who can work things out with you outside of the bedroom, and to make sure that you're mentally healthy.

It Will Not Bring Happiness

Just like anything in life, the only key to happiness is the way you think about your life. Thinking that going into D/s or becoming a submissive will bring you happiness is only going to backfire. Finding happiness could be as simple as taking a vacation, spending more time connecting with your friends and family, or simply focusing on your health. As mentioned above, if you're having depressive thoughts or relationship issues - you should be consulting a therapist or your partner instead.

So do you think that you're fit to be a submissive? Here are some questions you might want to first consider:

Do you wish to be in this type of relationship 24/7?

Perhaps you only wish to be a submissive during the scenes. Maybe you want to roleplay only during certain times. There are many ways this activity can be done, but you have to figure out what is right for you. Being in this role 24/7 means you're committing your mind, body and soul to it completely - not just for some nights only.

Are you prepared to surrender full control of your life to someone else?

This is a relationship involving total power exchange (TPE), where, for an indefinite duration, a submissive surrenders full control to the Dominant (sometimes referred to as Master/Mistress in a TPE relationship). 24/7 submissives do this, and they're commonly referred to as slaves.

With full control, it would mean that your Dominant decides what music you listen to, what clothes you wear, what perfume you use. Every decision belongs to your Dominant, including your hairstyle down to the very way you walk. You will even need permission to eat at the table with your Dominant.

On the other hand, roleplaying would mean entering into a D/s relationship only for an agreed upon time when the Dominant would have total control. Once the scene (a specific period of BDSM or D/s activity) is over, everything returns to normal.

Are you willing to please your Dominant anytime, anywhere?

Many come into this lifestyle looking to be used sexually, to service their Dominant at His/Her whim. Therefore, the submissive should not expect any reciprocation. Do not expect that you'll be able to escape out of the situation with an excuse.

Becoming a submissive creates a lifestyle, one that is completely of your choice and not something that has been forced unto you.

And if you understand and think you can handle that, then you're *almost* ready.

To keep you safe, let's set up some ground rules first.

Guidelines and Safety

There are a set of guidelines or codes of conduct that you can follow to ensure that you are safe and informed. These guidelines should be discussed with your Dominant, and any other parties involved in the relationship, roleplay, or scene, before it happens, to ensure that everyone is on the same page, which is very important because of the potentially dangerous acts that can happen during D/s. You cannot assume that another person has the same belief, tolerance or understanding as to what is considered safe and acceptable.

In the BDSM community, the oldest code of conduct is SSC (Safe, Sane and Consensual), which states that any safe, sane, and consensual action between adults is okay.

However, SSC has been seen as flawed because "safe" and "sane" is very subjective, and some activities may be "safe" for some people, but not for others.

Because of that, the RACK (Risk-Aware Consensual Kink) code of conduct was born. By establishing a spectrum of "safe" and "sane", understanding that what may be acceptable to one person may not be to another, the RACK code of conduct allows for more behaviors that others might deem as "edge play". There is no "safe" or "not safe" within RACK, only "safer" and "less safe."

There are newer codes of conduct, such as PRICK (Personal Responsibility Informed Consensual Kink) and CCC (Committed Compassionate Consent) that were created to try and fill up missing elements in SSC and RACK, both of which did not acknowledge personal responsibility and emotional well-being.

No matter which acronym you choose to guide you, consent is the most important part, which is why it's in all of the acronyms above. Remember that submission involves the submissive first *allowing* the Dominant to take control, not the Dominant *taking* control from the submissive.

Other than consent, communication is also crucial to ensure that all those involved are on the same page, that they understand each other, and that they know each other's limits. Never assume that the other party will know what your limits are if you don't tell them beforehand. Never assume that

Here are five other assumptions that you should not carelessly make.

1) Never assume that your partner(s) will know your limit, or that you will know theirs.

2) Never assume that experience is important to begin in D/s - everyone starts somewhere.

3) Never assume that experienced partner(s) will always be good partner(s).

4) Never assume that your partner(s) will look out for YOUR safety.

5) Never assume that a contract or a safe word would definitely keep you safe.

As such, it is important to always agree on a set of guidelines with your Dominant and all adults involved. If you don't know the person or the safety guidelines that they believe in - it's advisable not to get involved with them intimately if you don't feel comfortable doing so.

In BDSM, one of the most basic ways of ensuring your own safety, especially when you're with a new partner, is to use safewords. A safeword is a predefined "code word" that when used by a submissive, can cease the activity at hand if the submissive feels it has crossed a boundary, or become more than he or she can handle. Safewords are usually employed during times like resistance play, where struggling and resisting is part of the activity, and where the submissive saying "no" may not truly want to stop. In these cases, it's helpful to use a predetermined word that is unlikely to come up during a roleplay scene, but indicates the genuine desire to stop.

The most basic safewords used among beginners in BDSM are "green", "yellow" and "red" from the traffic light safeword system. Essentially, "green" means *This is great, please continue*", "yellow" means *This is okay, but please slow down*", and "red" means *STOP!*". Of course, you can decide to use other safewords - just discuss and agree on this with your Dominant beforehand.

Never rush into something that will compromise your safety.

Think about what you are doing, figure out what you want, and educate yourself. Read up on D/s, talk to people and gather as much information as you can to really get an idea of what you like and don't like. If there are people who really resonate with you and how you want to be - talk to them.

Go as slow as you need to and it's always okay to change your mind at any point if you're not feeling comfortable. Never feel pressured to continue, and never be afraid to just stop. Nothing good comes out of forcing yourself to stay in a situation that you no longer want to be in.

Remember - you've got plenty of time to do this right. It's always better to be sure than not sure enough.

Finding the right Dom

When you're searching for a Dominant, make sure you've done enough research so that you'll be able to do the following:

1. Pick a Dominant who you truly feel comfortable serving.

2. Set boundaries at the beginning before you begin a D/s relationship.

3. Obey as you promised, and do as you are asked. Nothing more, nothing less.

4. Be honest, loyal and trustworthy.

5. Communicate openly when asked; ask permission otherwise.

As a start, have a "Submissive Owner's Manual" to ensure that you and your Dominant are on the same page:

A submissive Owner's Manual

i need to feel safe

i need to know You accept me for all i am

i need to have clearly defined limits

i need You to be consistent

i need to expand my limits

i need You to teach me

i need goals

i need to be corrected

i need You to be my role-model

i need Your approval and reassurance

i need to be able to express myself

i need to learn from my mistakes

i need forgiveness when i fail You

i need to feel i contribute

i need to enjoy successes

i need to share with You

i need to feel loved, respected, and protected in Your ownership

The next question is, "How well do you need to know someone before submitting"?

Going into a D/s relationship as a submissive is inherently going to be more risky for obvious reasons. While terrible things could be done in such relationships, most people are basically good. Just take everything with a grain salt, and be cautious while keeping your eyes and mind open and alert.

Having said that, one good way to minimize risk is to venture into as many places as possible - be it online, communities, or munches (informal social meetings for those involved in or attracted to BDSM). Just mingle around and make as many friends as possible.

If you do meet a potential Dominant privately, and you've never met Him or Her before, try to set it up at a public place and set up a safe call with a trusted friend so that there will be someone who knows where you are and who you are meeting. A good Dominant would oblige and even let you take a photo of their ID to be sent to your safe call. This is for your security and peace of mind. Should the potential Dominant be reluctant or if you feel uncomfortable, it's best to trust your gut instinct and avoid the meetup completely.

Of course, the potential Dominant could send you a fake ID or licence registration. There will always be a risk whenever you meet someone new, whether it be in dating or even selling something on Craigslist. Heck, there will always be a risk even if you've met the person before numerous times. It's up to you if you want to take that risk.

If you're unsure or uncomfortable with the potential danger and risk associated with meeting someone in person, then don't. There's nothing wrong with taking the time to become acquainted with someone online or over the phone. You may be ready to meet someone only after knowing them for a day, week, months, or even years. Whatever it is, only meet someone in person when you are 100% comfortable and have safety measurements in place.

Once you've made the decision to meet a potential Dominant, it's time to find out if He or She is the right one for you.

Here are some example of questions you can ask your potential Dominant to really get to know them better:

"Are You single or married?"

"What experiences have You had?"

"What do You want in a submissive?"

"Are You in D/s as a lifestyle, for a hook up, just part-time or simply trying it out?"

"Have You ever collared someone and, if so, why were they released?"

In a way, it's kind of like a job interview and, in that sense, you really do want to know if it's a relationship that can work out in the long term. Just like in job interviews, you need to look out for qualities that will make a good Dominant.

Below is a good summary of the good and the bad qualities to look out for in a Dominant:

Good	Bad
Polite and sociable no matter what	Rude and/or abusive
Guides and teaches you	Know-it-all
Allows you to give control	Tries to take control
In full control of emotions	Unable to control anger
Designs a relationship based on your needs	Tries to fit you into a mold that He/She has created

Most importantly, a good Dominant will honor the decision of submissive should they decide to end the dynamic. This is not slavery - you make the final decision.

Remember this: You are the one in charge.

Final tips

Find good people to be your mentor - preferably someone who you aren't in a relationship with. This could be someone who is a Dominant or even other submissives. Basically, ensure that they are there to teach and guide you into becoming a better submissive.

Reading and researching will help you get a good understanding of everything that happens in the BDSM and D/s world. Go through as many forums and topics as you need to be a 100% sure that this is something you want to experience and immerse yourself in.

Lastly, set up boundaries where needed and don't be pressured to move too quickly into a relationship - wait till you're 100% comfortable.

If you've made that first step into becoming a submissive, we can now dive into how you can become better at it.

Becoming a Good Submissive

As the old adage goes, "Practice makes perfect". That's no exception in D/s relationships.

Once you've understood all the guidelines and safety values from the chapter before, you'll realize that you should always be in charge (even though you're the submissive). In the bedroom, that will of course change.

Lastly, it is crucial to understand that every Dominant is different and would have their own unique quirks, needs, wants and desires. Therefore, a lot of open communication, honesty and mutual respect is required between you and your Dominant to find out each other's likes, dislikes, limits, and requirements.

With all that out of the way, let's move on to the action list.

Follow Rules and Protocols

As a submissive, you serve and serve only for one purpose: your Dominant.

Other than the aforementioned safety guidelines that you and your Dominant would set before beginning the relationship, there are also rules and protocols that your Dominant might set for you to follow.

Such rules and protocols are used because they:

- Create a well-defined distinction between the Dominant and the submissive

- Provide a suitable foundation for the D/s relationship

- Clearly clarify how the submissive should serve the Dominant and behave in various circumstances

- Strengthen the connection between the Dominant and the submissive by differentiating them and their distinctive connection from others.

Typically, these rules are meant to regulate the submissive's conduct, communication and exchanges. Protocols can range from being very simple to being very detailed. They can establish the particular fashion in which certain roles must be performed in. For example in speech where a submissive must address the Dominant as "Master/Sir", or "Mistress/Miss". Some Dominants may even prefer to be called something else such as "Daddy", "My Queen", or "Princess".

However, the more specific the protocols are, the more challenging they may be to enforce. This may create a problem, for example, they may become hard to track or hard for the Dominant to recognise and amend all errors

Ideally, the rules must be clear and concise to establish a more general type of conduct and subservience that may be inferred and applied to various situations. This would be something that you as a submissive should consider when reviewing the protocol, to ensure that you'll be able to please your Dominant in the best way possible.

Here are some key points to note in each D/s relationship:

General Behaviour

The submissive exists to satisfy and serve the Dominant at any time in any situation. This suggests that the submissive must constantly consider the Dominant's wants and needs. The submissive should never reveal any signs of anger, frustration, disagreement or be disruptive in action or mind. All orders, requests, and commands must be duly acknowledged and meticulously executed.

Other basic submissive traits include but are not limited to:

- accepting the leadership of your Dominant with grace

- pleasing your Dominant by giving in to His/Her control

- willingly carrying out tasks (sexual or non-sexual) established by your Dominant.

- doing exactly as you're told, if you're expected to obey

- being respectful, reliable and honest

- being responsible for your actions

- avoiding being a problem or starting unnecessary/unwanted drama

- being transparent in all your dealings with your Dominant such as your feelings, worries boundaries, fantasies, and thoughts

- being able to speak up when necessary and not just tell your Dominant what you believe e/She will want to hear.

Other Rituals

Besides the submissive traits mentioned above, here are some other behaviors that you might consider adding into your protocol:

- daily morning check-ins

- removing your Dominant's shoes

- kissing your Dominant's feet

- massages

- fetching

- playing with toys

- controlling orgasm

- asking what you should wear

- asking if private areas should be groomed

- asking for permission in general, for every task or errand

- giving your Dominant control over all (or parts) of your daily life

Once again, the submissive's primary objective is to please his/her Dominant. However, the level of control you give to your Dominant partner is unique to each individual, so you might not be comfortable with total control. Whatever it is, the decision is yours to submit as much or as little of your daily life to your Dominant.

Sometimes, your Dominant might not be ready for that much responsibility. Take it as slow as you need to so that neither of you are overwhelmed. And never feel bad if you never give up much control at all.

Communication

Secondly, the submissive needs to have the ability to speak freely and truthfully about his or her emotions and thoughts, while still being respectful. This applies to all opinions, needs, beliefs, desires, and how you respond and react.

This allows honesty and open communication and once established, it should stay consistent as long as the submissive doesn't stop communicating with honesty. To not interconnect is to jeopardize your physical and emotional well-being.

Communication can be nonverbal, as long as what need to communicate gets across to your Dominant. For example, opening up in your journal, and then "telling" your Dominant through your journal entry is still considered an acceptable form of communicating.

Speech:

Further to communication, there are mannerisms and/or other behaviors that are expected of a submissive, for example:

"Showing respect"

First and foremost, the submissive is required to speak to the Dominant and other non-submissives using the proper honorifics. The Dominant must be addressed in the way that He/She prescribed, such as "Master" or "my Master", "Sir", or "my Owner". The submissive should also refer to him/herself as the "slave", "this slave", "Your property", or simply "he/she/it".

"Asking for permission"

The submissive must ask for the Dominant's permission before doing anything - from sitting, using the washroom, eating, and before reaching orgasm. For instance, instead of the submissive saying "I am coming", he/she would be required task for permission and use proper honorifics– "Sir, would it please Sir if this slave orgasmed, Sir?" or "Can I cum, Master?"

"Showing Gratitude"

Submissives must thank their Dominants for giving them the opportunity to serve. In sexual conduct, it is often mandatory that the submissive thank the Dominant for the orgasm that he/she was allowed to have.

"Using Specific Vocabulary"

Some Dominants may be more pedantic about this, and it could just be a subtle difference between "Can I be whipped now, Sir?" versus "May slave be whipped now, Sir?". Either way, your Dominant would correct you on this, should He/She decide to.

"Enunciation"

It's not always about *what* you say, but *how* you say it as well. A simple "Yes Sir" or "No Sir" must always be said with delight and without any hint of reluctance or displeasure.

Interaction

Sometimes, the D/s interaction extend outside of the bedroom and the submissive may be required to do things in public to please his/her Dominant. This is often the case in 24/7 or lifestyle D/s relationships.

For instance, when entering into the presence of the Dominant, the submissive might be obligated to announce his/her presence with a curtsy or bow. This is meant to acknowledge the submissive's status and his/her readiness to serve the Dominant. Depending on the circumstances and the

Dominant's discretion, the submissive could also be required to be either standing or kneeling when greeting the Dominant.

In general, it is quite practical in public setting to let your Dominant know where you are. This streamlines fetching, carrying, and any other duties you must attend to. It will also prevent bumping into one another while walking or mingling.

Implementation

Protocols provide a reliable way to establish the behaviors, communication, and interaction of a submissive. Starting out simple is always good as it's difficult and impractical to construct a complete set of protocols from scratch.

Adjustments and additions can happen over time. Taking advantage of the example set by other existing protocols would be good if you're just getting started.

Ensure that the rules, roles and duties are completely outlined and understood. Walk thought them and practice together to make any needed changes along the way, and amend errors when they happen. This process is referred to as "protocol training" or just "training".

It could be tiresome at the beginning as you, the submissive is still learning to become proficient with the protocol. However, with practice, you'll soon be consciously self-correcting and taking great pride in following the protocol and rules. A protocol is never static after all, and will evolve into something to suit the D/s relationship.

Practice makes perfect and as long as you (the submissive) do your best to follow protocol in order to please your Dominant, half the battle to becoming a good submissive is won.

Maintaining Submission Even When Apart

Being a good submissive isn't always about serving sexually or being present 24/7. With the help of technology, maintaining most of the aforementioned rituals and behaviors is very possible between submissives and Dominants who are apart, and even those who have a purely online relationship.

Here are some ideas to maintain submission even when you're apart:

- **Texting or Emailing**

   Daily rituals, check-ins, asking for permission, and using honorifics, should all be maintained dutifully through the phone, email, or any other means of communication at all. This could extend to everything and anything - asking your Dominant for permission on what to wear, eat, do, or go. Your Dominant can control your schedule, command you not to masturbate, or demand that you send an update every hour and you, as the submissive, must obey.

- **Journaling / Blogging**

   All your thoughts and feelings on submission, areas of sexual interests, fantasies, and anything else that pops into mind should be written down. This keeps yourself accountable for your Dominant, and He/She will be able to know what you're thinking, even when you're halfway across the globe.

- **Taking Pictures**

Similar to journaling, the more visual aspect would be to take pictures of what you're wearing everyday, even if it's just pyjamas, or anything at all that your Dominant wants.

- **Video Chat**

Better yet, use Facetime, Skype or Google Hangouts to call your Dominant to check in with Him/Her. Your Dominant may also give you commands and even enforce punishments over video chat. For example, your punishment may be to kneel on tiled floor in front of the camera while your Dominant watches or goes about His/Her daily life. As a good submissive, you will obey even without your Dominant being physically there.

Conditioning

As kinky as this book may be, there is a bit of science and psychology to it, especially if you're after proven methods on how to become better at something. Hence, we'll talk about conditioning.

Conditioning is a behavioral method where positive reinforcement, in the form of stimuli or rewards, is used to inspire a particular desired response within a certain situation. This is much needed in D/s relationships and you're probably already thinking that this might be something you'll actually have to learn in great detail.

Think about these examples:

1) Conditioning leather would make it soft and comfortable to wear while fortifying it against the elements and making sure it lasts a long time.

2) Conditioning a soldier usually means undergoing physical training until he has a body fit for battle. This is both mental and physical strengthening, training it to accept and follow orders - and to resist fear of death.

This works the same way as you embark on the journey to becoming a better submissive.

There are two main types of conditioning that will help:

Classical Conditioning

This is best understood using the example of Pavlov's dog.

Every time the scientist rings the bell when he feeds the dog, an association is created between the ringing sound and the expectation that food would arrive.

As such, whenever the dog heard the bell, it would begin to salivate. This becomes a conditioned response.

So in BDSM for example, a particular toy can be regularly used in conjunction with sexual pleasure, then the sight or feel of that toy will eventually start to elicit a sexual arousal response, even if it is not a sexual toy.

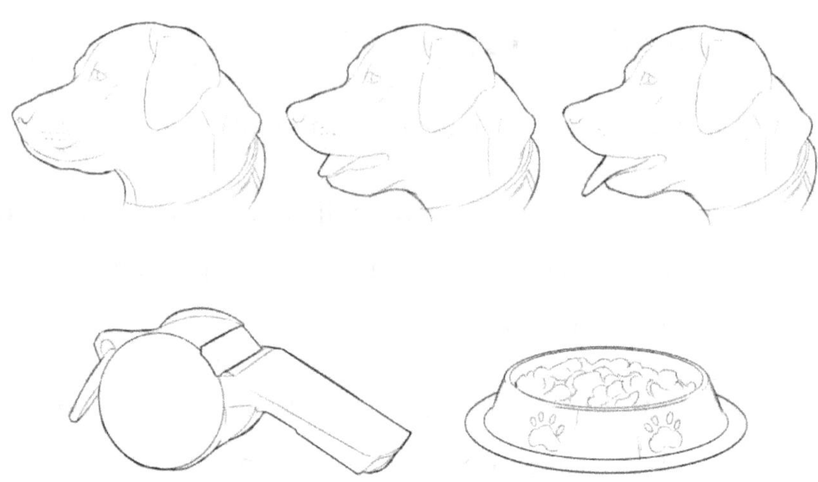

These physical conditioned responses can be used in various ways. One really simple way is to simply speed things up. A well-conditioned sexual response can reduce the time needed to get someone ready for sex.

Alternatively, it can be used to tease and torment the submissive in public. For example, a negative association can be used in place of punishment in a public place. A conditioned response to a finger snap that is usually associated with a negative sensation can get the attention of the submissive very quickly and will effectively let them know they are in trouble. Any and all senses can be used for this. Smell, touch, taste, sight, and sound. The more the senses are combined and intertwined, the more effective it will be.

When possible, you want the stimulus to be something rarely encountered in day to day life. You'd want your Dominant to have as much control over the stimulus as possible, so He/She should be the only one to provide that stimulus so no overlap occurs should someone or something else replicates it.

If it's to link a trigger word to your orgasm, it better not be a word you hear regularly each day, otherwise it will never work.

Operant Conditioning

The next type of conditioning is usually what people think of when a submissive is being trained as it's related to rewards and punishments. This is everything a Dominant does to encourage or discourage certain behaviors of the submissive, whether intentional or not.

This includes Their body language, facial expressions, the words They use when you talk to Them, if They use your real name or your pet name, whether They look at you when talking, and pretty much every other thing the Dominant would do.

An example of this would be the etiquette that is taught to us early on as kids by our teachers or parents. When someone gives you a gift, you say "thank you" automatically -- that's conditioning. And it doesn't take long for our brains to pick up on these patterns quickly and adapt to them. In fact, teachers can usually train a room full of students to comply with how they prefer to run the class, either encouraging questions and discussion, or silent note-taking -- all within the first day of school.

Essentially if you want to effectively train anyone, whether a Dom, a sub, or even your friends - you just have to be consistent in your actions to let them know what is expected of them and what they can expect from you. And you never have to explicitly provide instructions or direction - that's the beauty of effective training.

Becoming a good submissive is definitely not a game, nor is it a short-term means to an end. Something like this - psychological conditioning - will have long-term and long lasting impact on people.

It takes years of conditioning to say "thank you" and greet people by shaking their hands. In a D/s relationship, it's pretty much the same. It'll become a huge part of you and your personality.

As a good submissive, be prepared to let your Dominant take full responsibility of your psychological well-being until the moment the D/s relationship comes to an end.

How to Increase Pain Tolerance?

The first thing you need to know about pain is that if you are a submissive or learning about submission, and you don't like pain or don't think you like pain then that doesn't mean you aren't submissive - it just means you aren't a masochist. There are many pathways to being a submissive, but inflicting pain into submission is just one of the possibilities.

It is very possible to avoid this altogether and even go into service, domestic, or even animal play. Sado-masochism is sometimes included in D/s relationships, but it doesn't mean a D/s relationship has to involve physical pain. Having said that, if this isn't up your alley - you can skip this chapter altogether.

There are many ways to increase pain tolerance otherwise, and that's through a lot of learning and practicing. It is recommended that you practice these the next time you play and see what works best for you.

Breathing

Breathing steadily has long been a medical approach used to reduce pain, and this technique is widely used and proven as a great distraction during childbirth. Researchers believe that "slowing breathing has a direct impact on the sympathetic nervous system, which helps control blood flow and skin temperature, blocking some of the pain response."

Pretense

Imagining a fantasy as you experience pain can provide a distraction, or an enhancement of that pain, depending on what you choose to imagine. Fantasizing that the pain you are experiencing is only happening in a dream where suffering is natural can allow your body to withstand the suffering until it is ready to process it. It's actually common to drop this act altogether once your body can process pain in other more beneficial ways.

Visualization

Similar to pretense, this is another distraction method where you think of pain as something tangible to your senses.

You can:

1) See the pain as light that can be dispersed throughout your body. For example, if you receive a whip to the back, you can visualize it as light flashing across your skin and branching into several smaller flashes to the rest of the body, it will mentally spread the pain, making it more tolerable.

2) Visualize heat instead of light to spread the pain across your skin. Just like certain alcohol rubs, you can even imagine this to be that of a similar warm/cool sensation - something more soothing rather than excruciating.

3) Add color to visualizing light - possibly even imagine rainbows of color radiating from the point of pain if you want to be creative. From white to red to yellow, green and blue - each color would lessen the pain until it's dissipated and gone.

Storage

It is possible to try and hold the discomfort for long as possible, and then ask permission from your Dominant as you release it- by trembling, shrieking, laughing, squirming, or stomping. Whatever works best for you. Moving this energy through your body can somehow disperse the pain, which is why you hear guys being told to "shake it off" after being hit in the nuts by a foreign object.

Eroticize pain

During sensual play, the Dominant can also mix in some pain – clitoral stimulation at the same time as pinching nipples, or spanking interspersed with orgasms. Basically anything sexual and erotic to mix in the sensual response with the response to pain. This comes back down to the basic Pavlovian conditioning of association.

Crying

This is almost quite self-explanatory - tears are actually a normal release of emotions. This could be from the pain you are enduring or from bottled up emotions that all of a sudden come to the surface during play.

Laughing

For some people, there's a different way to cope with negative emotions and one of them is through laughing. As silly as it sounds, there is an actual chemical change in our bodies that helps to ease pain and release stress. These are endorphins.

In a nutshell, laughing helps to positively release that stress and encourages the body to improve overall pain tolerances.

Encountering a (physical) limit

Sometimes you just have to let the situation happen organically. Imagine you and your Dom playing and happily enjoying what is going on between the two of you. As the scene continues you begin to feel that you're reaching your peak tolerance, but you continue to play. Then, almost without warning you hit a wall and is forced to yell the safe word.

You've just hit a limit - and this is not necessarily a bad thing. This could be a temporary limit and if you feel that you hit this too soon, it's possibly due to other stress or issues you are dealing with. If you're new at this, the limit could just be a new-found hard or soft limit; an edge of play for you to know what kind of boundaries you have.

Either way the results are normal and sometimes shocking; it's important to know that some can be breached while others are solid walls of our boundaries. All you need to do is learn from the experience and grow in play and pain.

Overcoming the false edge (psychological)

Contrary to actually encountering the limit. There are times when you are playing with pain and you reach a moment where you think only of wanting it to stop, but the pain you are feeling isn't why you are considering it.

It could be the fear or uncertainty of what could come next in which, is known as the false edge.

The false edge isn't a physical limit, but a sense that you are going to lose control if you continue. What's really happening is you fear letting go of the last bit of control that you have which is the control over your reactions. This, in the world of

Sado-masochism, may not be the most pleasurable act possible.

If you want to please your masochist Dominant, then you must go beyond your false edge to reach your true edge. A person past the false edge will begin to start reacting instinctively rather than in a controlled method. This is a far more relaxed and freer feeling that you might realize.

One way to get past this is really just to talk and learn to fully trust your Dom, that you're in capable of hands that are well aware of your pain tolerance and any other concerns you may have.

If something is too much, it is important to discuss and build up to the activity gradually bit by bit. First and foremost - communication should be the most important thing.

SEXUAL POSITIONS FOR D/S RELATIONSHIPS

It is generally safe to say that in a D/s relationship, the positions (sexual and non-sexual) are the ways a Dominant prefers their sub to stand, kneel etc. In this segment, we'll only be looking at sexual positions, which may overlap with some non-sexual ones due to the versatility of these positions. For the most part, as long as the sexual position allows the Dom to take full or partial control of the sub in a manner that He/She is satisfied with, then it can be considered to be a good, D/s position.

Not everyone uses formalized positions in general, but there are basic ideas of what they are and many of them might actually be a variance of another. It comes down to what your Dominant prefers and they can set your positions if He/She desires them. Here are some examples:

SUBMISSIVE TRAINING

Attention Positions:

- Standing/Waiting: legs spread moderately, hands clasped at the small of the back, head up, eyes lowered

- Inspect: hands clasped behind neck, head bowed

- Kneeling: legs parted, ankles crossed, back straight, head up, eyes lowered, arms crossed behind back

- Expose: legs parted, ankles crossed, back straight, head up, eyes lowered, arms behind neck

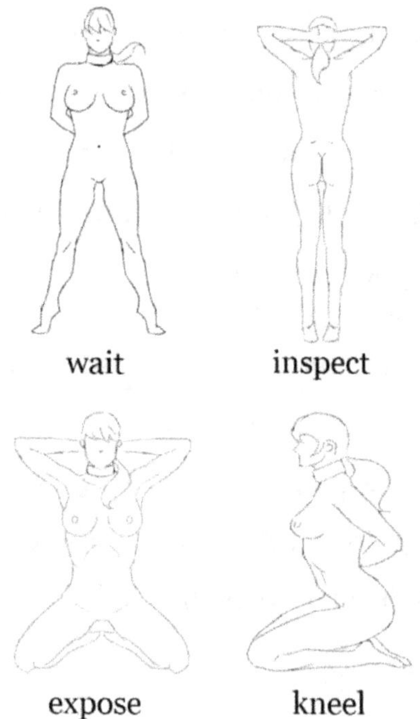

Spanking Positions:

- Floor: over the knee (OTK) with both hands and feet on floor

- Humble: facing away from Dominant, straddle His/Her thighs, bent from waist, hands flat to floor, back arched to raise buttocks

- Wall: facing with hands touching wall, body bent, arched back with buttocks raised until the back is parallel to the ground

- Rear: body bent over, hands on knees, buttocks raised

wall

rear

humble

floor

SUBMISSIVE TRAINING

Humiliating Positions:

- Endure: squat on toes, legs moderately spread, head up

- Hands: squat on toes, legs moderately spread, head up with hands arms raised

- Punishment: facing away from Dominant, straddle His/Her thighs, bent from waist, hands flat to floor, back arched to raise buttocks and feet raised up so weight is shifted mostly onto the knees

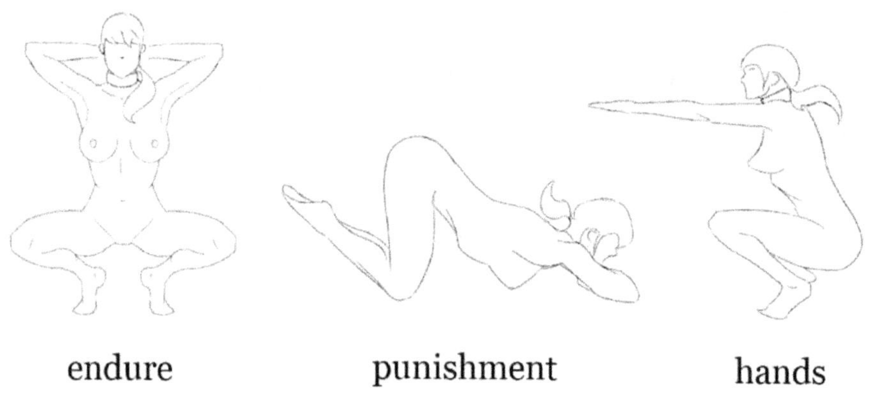

endure   punishment   hands

The positions shown above are just a few standard commands that are typically used by the Dominant for His/Her submissive. In most of those positions, you would notice that the Dominant is able to sexually arouse the submissive or engage in some form of sexual play.

And should the Dominant be kind enough, the submissive can take on the "Rest" position where he/she sits cross-legged, head down with hands covering the crotch region.

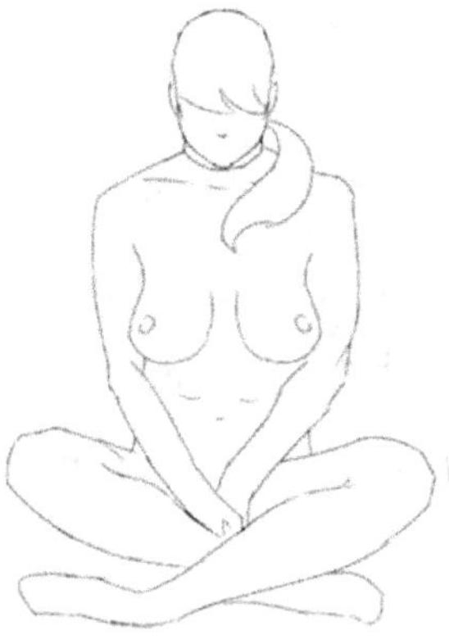

rest

Basic Bedroom Scenarios

With D/s relationships, any sexual position that gives the Dominant full control over His/Her submissive can be considered a good one.

It comes down to how experimental you are and what you prefer doing in that position. Some positions allow the Dominant to lock just the submissive's arms and neck, while others could even prevent them from moving whatsoever.

The Submissive

A slight variation from the doggy-style (still considered a good D/s position), "The Submissive" is when the submissive stands on one knee and leans forward as much as possible, bending her/his elbows and putting most of her/his weight there.

The Dominant is located behind His/Her submissive partner so that his/her stretched leg is between His/Her legs, one hand is placed on the hip of the submissive's leg, bent in knee, the other hand is on the back of the submissive, which He/She can stroke in the process. Female Dominants in this position may use a strap-on to penetrate Her female or male submissive.

The Marshmallow

"The Marshmallow" is a very comfortable position for oral satisfaction, and is quite versatile for some bondage, if preferred.

The submissive partner lies on his/her back, while the Dominant sits between the submissive's legs to embrace them, while orally pleasuring (or punishing) the submissive.

The Turtle

A somewhat more intricate variation from the doggy, the submissive kneels forward and presses his/her chest onto the knees. The Dominant partner then takes the submissive from behind while channelling His/Her weight onto the submissive, rendering the submissive quite helpless in terms of movement. Some bondage can also be used in this position.

Female Dominance

Female Dominance is the fetish where the Primary Woman is the one that's dominant, while their partner (either male or female) is submissive to their every whim. Often this is a major theme of BDSM related activities, and is a complete subversion of what's generally expected; where the male partner is dominant, and the woman is submissive.

Strap On Dildo

Strap on Dildo's are exactly as they sound. They're dildo's attached to a harness that the Female wears in an effort to simulate having a penis to use against their partners (Either male or female) and simulate penetration that a Female partner otherwise would not be able to simulate. This can be used as a form of dominance on a partner as well, as part of the Female Dominance Fetish.

Playing with Toys and Rope

While using toys isn't necessarily a part of D/s relationships, it is fairly common in making sexual positions more fun and exciting.

The Harness

A sex harness for example, provides some assistance for the Dominant to support and maneuver a submissive with less effort. Strong thigh leather straps and handles attached to the chest allow the Dominant to control the submissive's movements and enjoy weightless penetration in any position.

Nipple clamps, gag, ankle cuffs

Some toys are used to punish, like the gag or the nipple clamp. Sometimes it's simply to make control a lot easier, like the ankle cuffs.

The position demonstrated below shows how helpless the submissive can be with just a few extra sex toys.

Mastery – Suspended

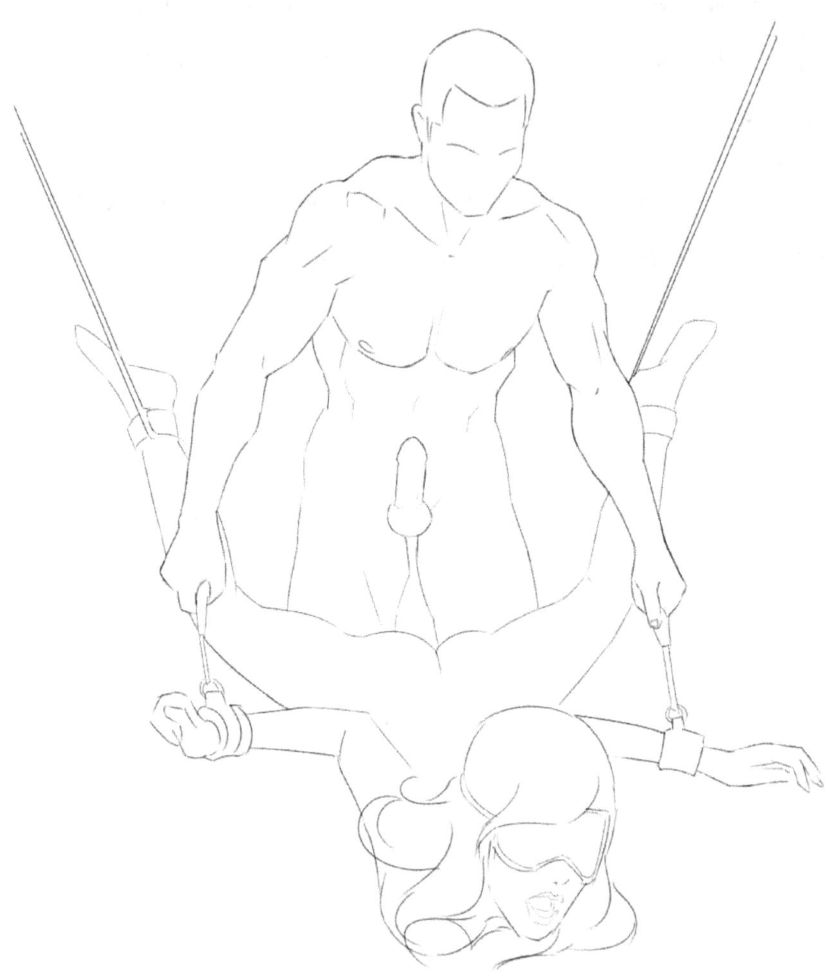

Another level beyond if you're a masochist is to get your Dominant to suspend you after being cuffed. This heavily restricts movement and can potentially cause a bit more pain for you to endure, which gives your Dominant a bit more pleasure.

Hogtie Bondage

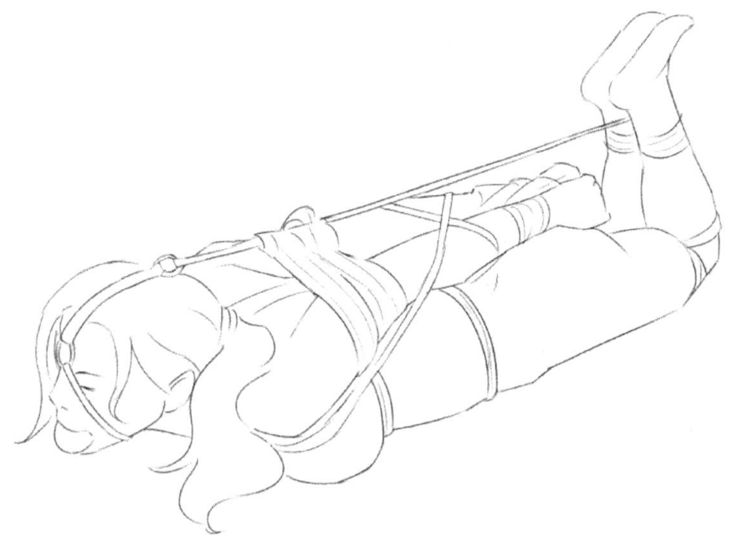

If you purely want to use rope, it'd help if you were in scouts, otherwise things may get a little complicated. This is known as hogtie bondage for obvious reasons, and will completely restrict movement for the submissive.

Only if you have 100% trust in your Dom, then are you advised to try something like this.

Simple Chair Tie-up

Similarly, tying a submissive down and jerking them off with a fleshlight would be great for Doms. This is great to use on male submissives and allows the Dominant to control the submissive's orgasm as well. A vibrator or dildo can be used on female submissives in this effect.

Tiptoe Crotch Rope Spreader Bar Strappado

The strappado position refers to any position where the arms are bound together behind the back and elevated.

It is crucial to note that the leverage of the arms can, in principle, dislocate the shoulders (which is how real-world torturers use it) so it is advised to use this very carefully. Under no circumstance should the submissive be suspended, but he/she can be severely punished in this position, or deeply penetrated.

Latex Fetish

Who doesn't like latex, and how smooth it can be? Latex Fetish's are from people who adore the feel and sound of latex on the skin, as it rubs back and forth, and constricts on the body in certain ways. Often the Latex outfits include various masks, harnesses, and tools and toys that are designed to tighten around the body.

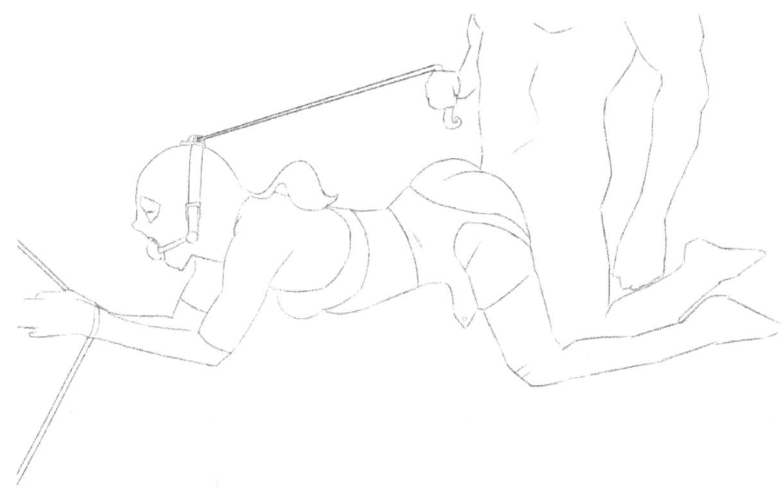

Roleplaying and Questionable Consent

While there's a fine line as to what's abhorrent (paedophilia, bestiality), there are grey areas which are very much legal and perfectly, socially acceptable.

For example, it's quite okay to dress up as a dog and have the submissive behave as a pet to serve the Dominant sexually. Here's an example of a position showing how:

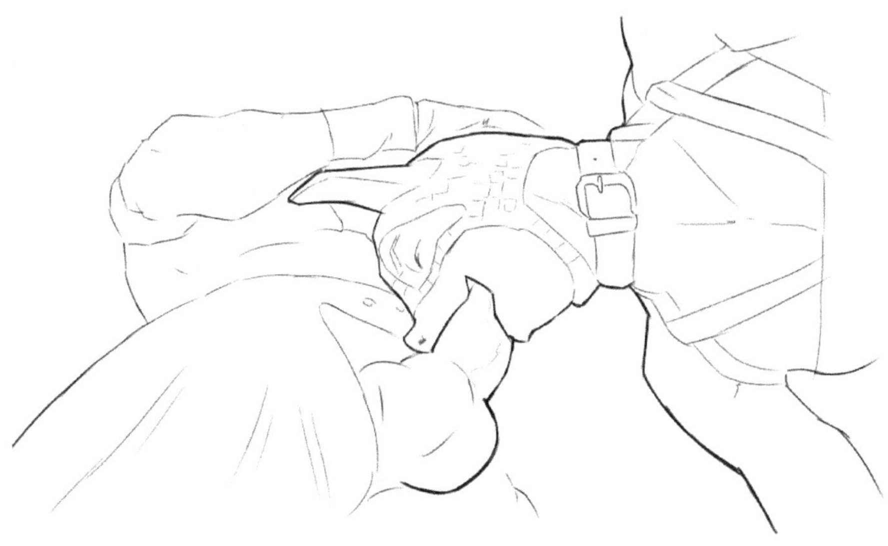

submissive Pet Play - submissive Partner dressed as a dog giving oral sex

submissive Female chained to a fence, and forcefully played with by her Dominant partner

(Genital) Torture Without Pushing Too Far

Besides bondage, there are other positions which give easy access for the Dominant to torture their submissives, either by pinching nipples, putting the penis in a cock cage or simply teasing the submissive's vagina. Here are some examples:

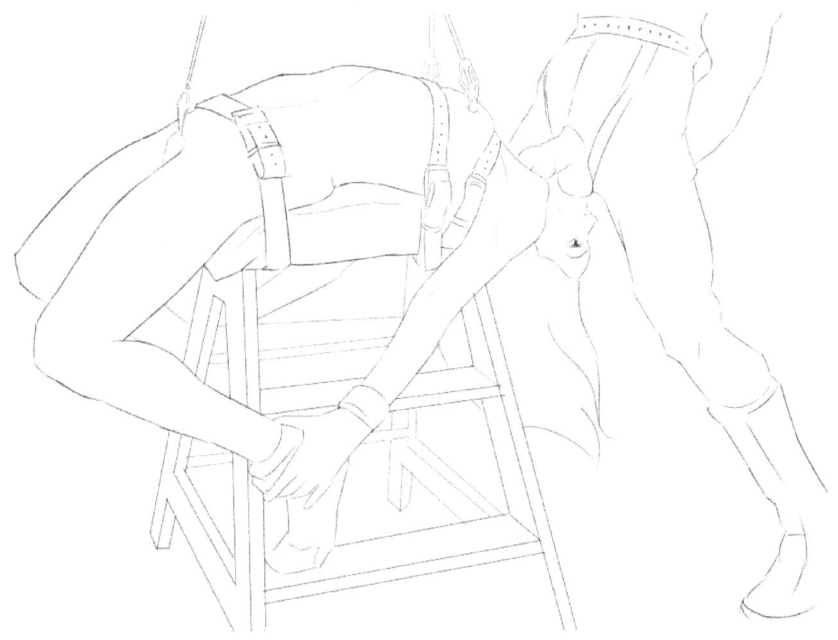

submissive Female harnessed on a BDSM horse giving oral sex to her Dominant partner

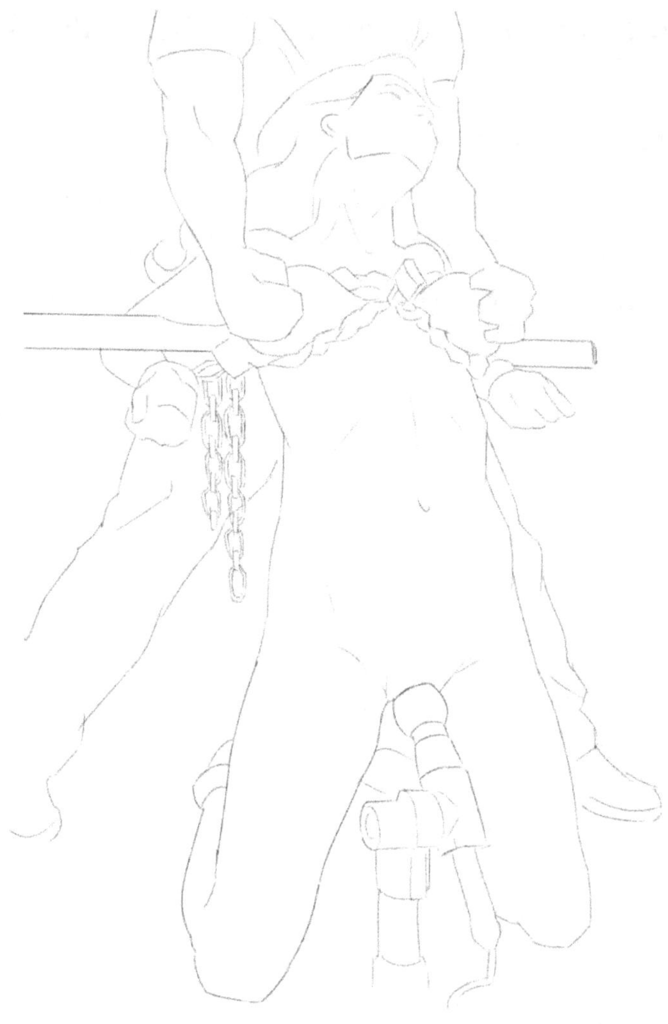

submissive Female harnessed down with chains, forced to straddle over a vibrator massager wand that stimulates the vaginal area

submissive Female tied up and forced on the tips of her toes to heighten arousal.

submissive Female tied and harnessed down while two Dominant partners engage in genital torture

submissive tied over a BDSM horse while two dominant partners engage in intercourse, and torture her nipples

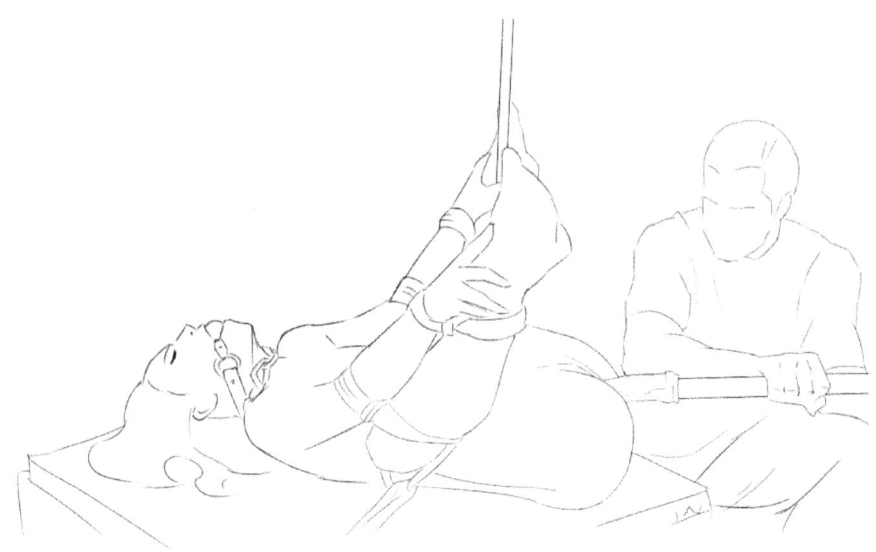

submissive Female hogtied down, with her vagina tortured with massive dildo to the brink of orgasm.

Suspension and Other Forms of Bondage

Suspension is also commonly used to control or restrict the movements of a submissive, which actually create a wide variety of sexual positions for a D/s relationship.

submissive harnessed to ceiling while engaging in oral with her Dominant partners

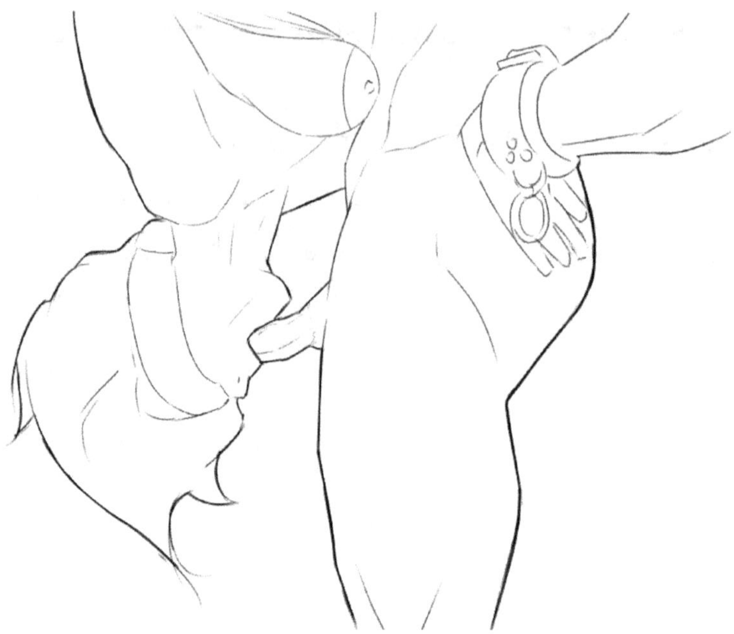

submissive Partner suspended upside down while engaging in oral, forcing blood to pool to her head to heighten arousal

submissive partner with her arms tied above her head engaging in intercourse with her partner, while being forced to stand.

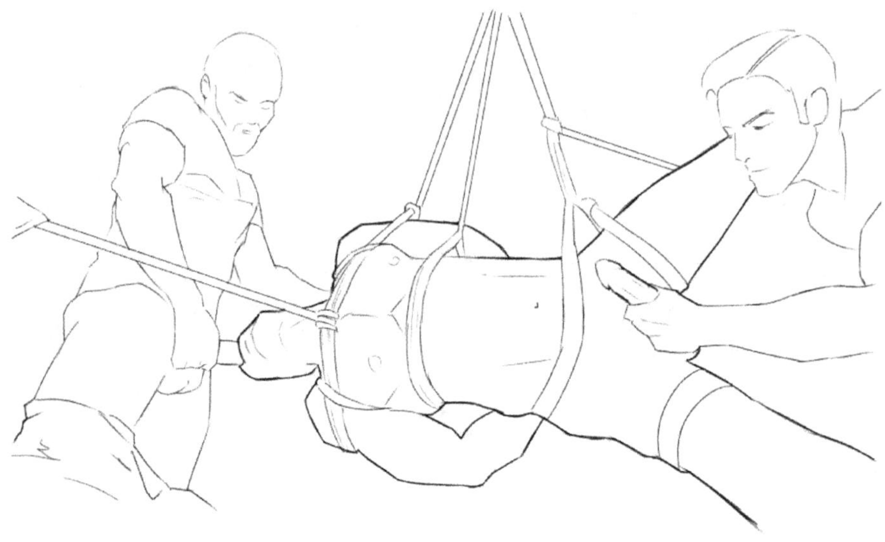

submissive male suspended on his side and bound while being forced to give oral to one Dominant Partner, while being stimulated by his other Partner

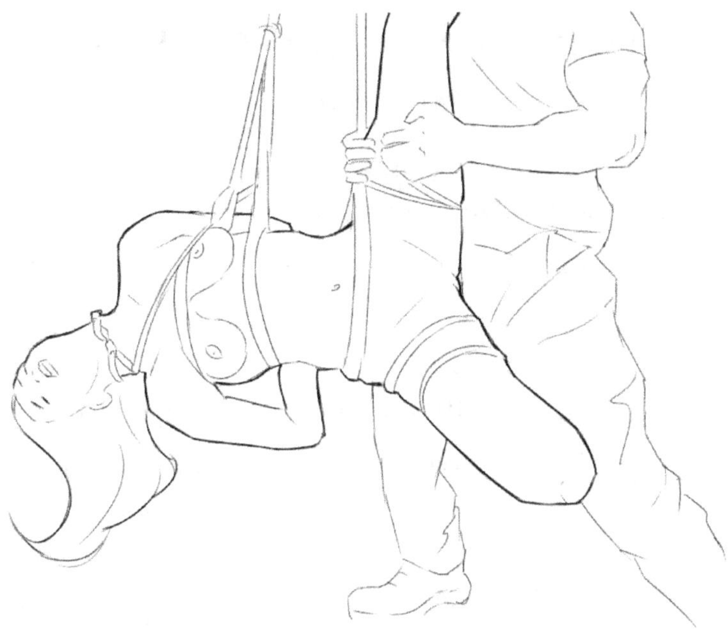

The Dominant partner having intercourse with one submissive while she's harnessed to the ceiling

Threesomes, Orgies and Gender Neutral Sessions

To finish off, while D/s relationships seem like it's just limited to a single Dominant to one submissive - this is hardly ever the case.

It's normal for a submissive to even have two Doms, or more commonly a Dom to have multiple submissives. Here are some positions in which they usually interact.

Bound submissive engaging in multiple partners both with intercourse, and with oral sex

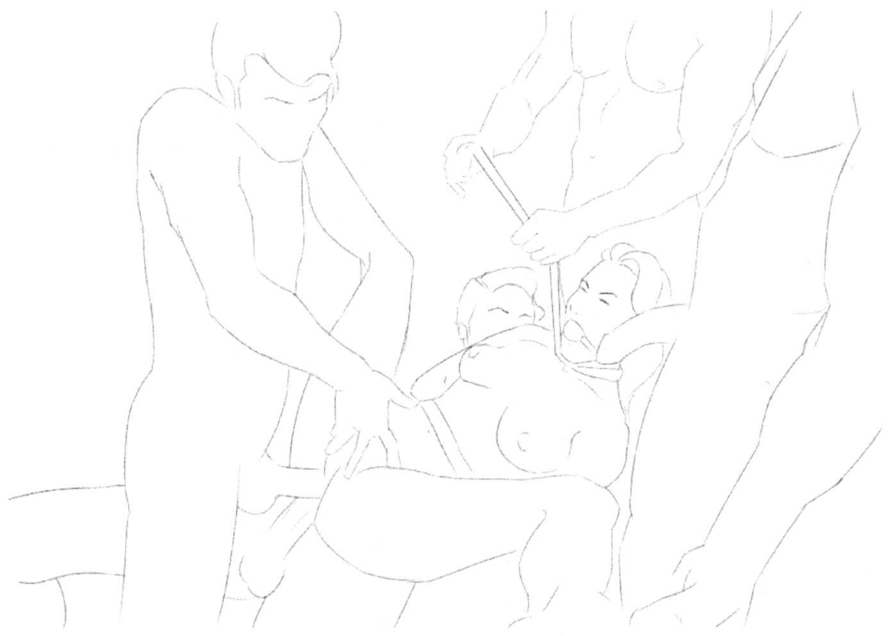

Bound and gagged submissive engaging in a "gangbang" with multiple partners at once

submissive Male bound, gagged, and engaging in genital torture with various clothed Dominant females

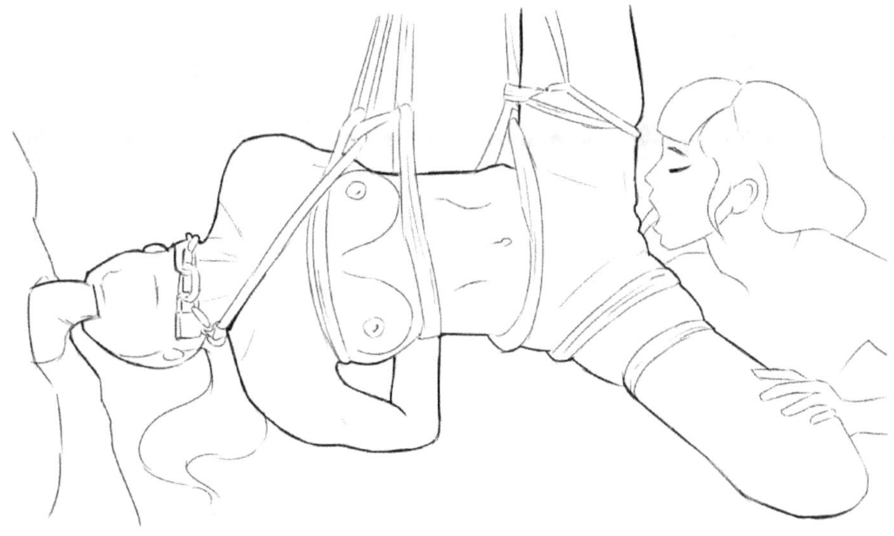

Bound and Suspended submissive engaging and engaged in oral sex both with her Dominant partner, and the secondary submissive

Two Dominant Partners engaging in both Oral and Penetration intercourse, forcing the submissives to pleasure one another for the Dominant's pleasure

CONCLUSION

The key takeaway for this book is that submission isn't a game, and it takes a lot of emotional and mental energy to become a good submissive. It's about always being at your best, to serve and be available for your Dom. You can't be lazy or selfish - and expect this to be a fantasy that's going to be fulfilled in one night. It takes month or even years to build a proper D/s relationship.

As such, communication and trust is important - both Doms and subs need to be able to respectfully talk to each other about their relationship. Aside from being Dom and sub, their relationship is quite similar to that of a typical one.

Having said that, it is also normal that there would be good and bad Doms, so you have to trust your gut about who you meet. Safety is a high priority, and remember that you are in charge about who you want to be subservient to. Be cautious and if something feels wrong, it probably is.

Don't go into D/s thinking it'll improve aspects of your life or well-being, not your sex life, relationships, career, etc. You should improve your overall state first, and then make D/s a bonus feature of your already awesome life.

Finding yourself may take time and as they say, "It's not about the destination, but the journey". Never let anyone force your submission, including yourself. Not everyone is meant to be a sub.

But hopefully this book would allow you to find yourself, test out what is possible and turn you into the best kind of submissive you ever hoped to be.